Clown Is Sick

Written by Jill Eggleton

Illustrated by Clive Taylor

PEARSON

This story is
about Clown.

The people in the book

Clown

The bus driver

The doctor

Clown came home from work.

He put his clown shirt on the chair.

He put his clown hair
on the lamp,
and he put his clown nose
on the bird's cage.

Then Clown went to bed.

In the morning,
Clown put on his shirt
and his hair and his nose.
But he sneezed.

Clown will...

go back to bed?

have breakfast?

Clown had breakfast
but he sneezed and sneezed!
His breakfast went
all over the kitchen.

Clown cleaned his teeth.
But he sneezed and sneezed.
Toothpaste went
all over the bathroom.

Clown went off to work.
He sneezed going down the road.
He sneezed on the bus.

He sat down by a woman and he sneezed and sneezed and

sneezed!

The bus driver stopped the bus.
He looked at Clown.

"You are sick," he said.
"You will have to go
to the doctor.
There is a doctor
in that house."

Clown got off the bus.
He went in to see the doctor.

"I'm very sick," he said.

And Clown sneezed and sneezed
and **sneezed!**

The doctor will look at...

Clown's ears?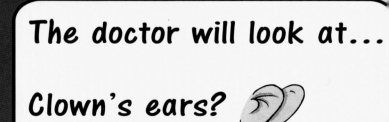

Clown's feet?

The doctor looked in Clown's ears.

"Your ears are OK," she said.

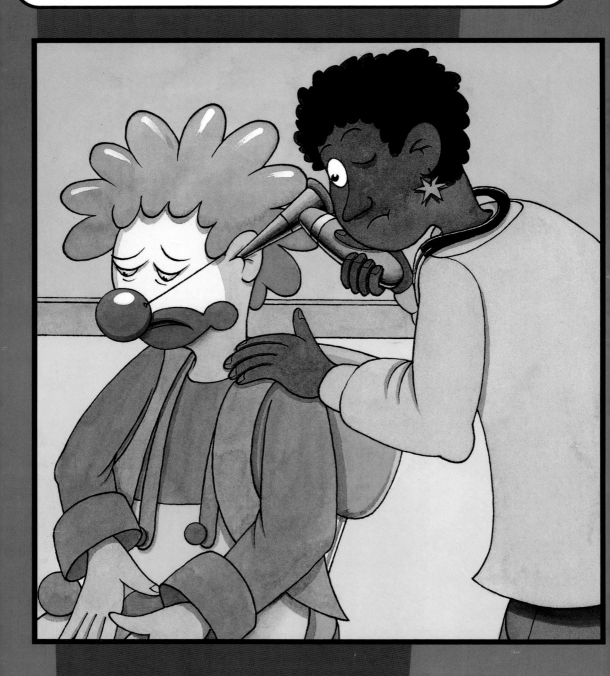

The doctor looked at Clown's tongue.

"**Your tongue is OK,**" she said.

The doctor looked at Clown's nose.

"Take off your nose," she said.

Clown took off his nose.

"I see," said the doctor.
"You are not sick."

"But I am sick," said Clown.
"I'm very sick!"

The doctor looked at Clown.

"No you are not," she said.

"But I have sneezed and sneezed and sneezed," said Clown.

"You will sneeze," said the doctor. "You will sneeze with a feather in your clown nose!"

The End

Story sequence

Did the story go like this?
Yes? No?

Did the story go like this?
Yes? No?

Word Bank

bed

breakfast

bus

cage

chair

ears

feather

hair

lamp

teeth

tongue

toothpaste